WHO KNOWS

Poems by

Jill Toulantas

First published by Busybird Publishing 2017

Copyright © 2017 Jill Toulantas

ISBN 978-1-925585-38-4

This book is copyright. Apart from any fair dealing for the purposes of study, research, criticism, review, or as otherwise permitted under the Copyright Act, no part may be reproduced by any process without written permission. Enquiries should be made through the publisher.

Cover design: Busybird Publishing
Layout and typesetting: Busybird Publishing

Busybird Publishing
PO Box 855
Eltham Victoria
Australia 3095
www.busybird.com.au

In loving memory

of my parents

and for

Regina

CONTENTS

The Stranger	1
Adolescent	2
Therapy	3
Bereavement (Haiku)	6
Woodwind	7
Family	8
Him	9
Match	10
Trophy	11
Shrinks	12
The Beggar	14
Ego	15
Contrast	16
Grief	17
Father	20
Hope	23
Sparrow	24
Torch	25
Status	26
Grit	27
Conned	28
Beauty	29
Gold	30
Delight	31
Solitaire	32
Companions	33
Me And Mine	34
Fools	36
Aftermath	37
Choice	38

Blanket	39
Chaos	40
Façade	42
Desire	43
Sage	44
Death's Door (Haiku)	46
Encounter	47
Whirlpool	48
Nirvana	49
Acme	50
Plunder	51
Eden	52
Keepsake	53
The Governess	54
Motherhood	57
Love	58
All Of Us	59
Sonnet (To My Mother)	60
Homecoming (Haiku)	61
Alphabet Poem 1 – Des(s)erts	62
Alphabet Poem 2 – Anew	63
Techno Fantasy	64
Retail Therapy	65
Who Knows	66
Regret	68
The Last Evening	70
Broken	72
Time Out	74
Waste Land	75
Exit	76

1946

*"Looking on my tiny self
Proudly from above."*

THE STRANGER

I saw him sitting in the train,
A face like his I'd never seen,
I knew I'd not see him again
Yet so entranced I'd never been.

His hair was thinning, grey and long,
His narrow body worn and old,
But in his eyes so kind and strong
There played a melody of gold.

I saw in him of what I'd dreamed,
Unblemished beauty of the heart,
A kindly countenance which beamed
A wisdom far too deep to chart.

I knew him not, we never spoke,
And stations later he was gone;
But I will not forget that bloke
Whose face on me so briefly shone.

1967

ADOLESCENT

A host of homeless feelings, thoughts and cravings,
A million mental spurts which dart and fade,
Threaded on a cord of nameless longing,
Is this the pointless mess of which I'm made?
What bliss if someone else could read my chaos,
Another heart and mind to fully care,
The more I live, the more I ache for contact,
The more I live, the more there seems to share.

If I could pool the energy together
That kindled since my birth my buzzing mind,
I'd have the tool with which to build a dwelling
Where man's frustration could no lodging find.

1967

THERAPY

At age eighteen she saw a man
To cure her depression;
He seemed a caring, kindly soul
Who gave a good impression.

Soon after she was sent into
A private institution,
A pleasant place, though asking
Much financial contribution.

She wasn't sick, just lost, bewildered,
Helpless how to live;
She hoped naively that her stay
Support and help would give.

Two weeks she spent in that huge home
Which housed a hundred cases,
Many hopeless victims, groping,
Madness in their faces.

Others simply sat around,
Smoking, lifeless, crying.
Someone had decided it was
Better there than dying.

She realized she was different,
She just needed contact badly
To resurrect the girl before
Life made her feel so sadly.

She waited for her doctor,
Simply longing for a talk.
But no, he sidestepped contact,
Would from conversation balk.

Instead he used a slick machine,
Yes, shock treatment was given.
All consciousness was wiped away,
Her mind to coma driven.

On waking there was nausea
And disorientation.
What happened and where was she?
Till she grasped the explanation.

Electric shocks day after day -----
"Well, aren't you feeling better?
When you came into hospital
You seemed somewhat upsetter."

Yes, she felt hopeful, much more cheerful
Than she had before;
But where'd the memory gone she had
When she came in that door?

So home she went, elated, manic,
Full of life again.
But no one knows how much those shocks
Abused and bruised her brain.

So many others stayed behind
With such a range of ills,
Psychiatrists, speechless, popping in,
Prescribing countless pills.

Once home she thought on what she'd seen,
She found a certain gladness.
But how can she forget that time,
The overwhelming sadness.

                                                  1968

BEREAVEMENT (Haiku)

Family fading, gone.
Piled things loiter pointlessly,
Desert doused in pain.

                                        1970

WOODWIND

My world;
Slender black pipe,
Intricate silver keys,
Troublesome double reed.

Its celestial sound
Soared over orchestras,
Blowing me heavenwards.
Intoxicating, hypnotic,
It kidnapped my being,
Becoming me.

                                                    1974

FAMILY

A godless religion
Is relayed to all,
The family, kin,
Society's core.

It neglects
The vast, varied family:
The spontaneous smile
Of a stranger in the street,
The unexpected touch
Of a passing traveller,
Anonymous hours shared
With unknown others,
Episodes of closeness
With chosen ones,
And deep, enduring friendship
That fills the cracks
In the pathways of our lives.

1975

HIM

Long ago there was a man
Whose soul stroked mine
Silently,
And stayed entwined
Through our separate lives.

Now, on his return,
That enduring thread
Ties me to him
With savage strength,
Fanned into full flower
Of feeling and fulfilment.
Love and light flood my life
Shed by the sheer beauty of his being.

                                                1982

MATCH

As a woman
In this world
I carried a dream,
A beautiful image,
Deeply personal.

It accompanied me
Through all my days,
Silently, secretly
Inside my soul.

It dwelt within
Without fruition
Till I found
You.

1982

TROPHY

"Win!"
Treacherous, tiny term.
Chimps chasing cheetahs,
Executives seek 'success'.
Like a brainwashed bullock,
A sportsman spurns defeat.

No family
Of fame or fortune,
True triumph opens
Nameless in obscurity.

An inner victory won,
The winner wakes
And we who watch and touch,
Feel the flare of inspiration,
Glimpse the glow from a happy heart.

1983

SHRINKS

An ageing kindly doctor has helped many beat the booze,
Has heard a million stories of those in life who lose.
He does his best for paranoiacs, many a melancholic,
Until at last he's finished for he was an alcoholic.

A small and almost unknown man sits sluggish on his chair.
You sit in front of him and wait while silence fills the air.
At last, embarrassed, hesitant, you tell why you feel bad;
But time is up, no words from him – just his prescription pad.

A soft and languid fellow shows you into his plush room.
This time he talks, but what he says makes apprehension loom.
By chance your hand strays near your heart --- "You're feeling something deeply."
"That's right I am, you're just a fool, a fraud who charges steeply!"

A young attractive doctor makes you hope he'll have a brain,
That you won't undergo the same experience again.
He leads you to his office, "Please sit down over there."
Oh not again, he's saying nothing; all he does is stare.
After fifteen minutes gone (a forty minute session),
Angrily you break the quiet, a much begrudged concession.
"I won't be back," you say to him. "I think your technique stinks.
Getting paid for silence!" You don't care what he thinks.

A tiny fat psychologist, his office lined with books,
Has presence, and intelligence and wisdom in his looks.
At last you've found a real one, at last – communicate –
But wait for it, that sharp man's mind is full of hang ups, hate.
The problems start when you've the gall to question what he states.

In rage he shouts "Just listen!" so you sweat there while he waits.
He speaks again, you clarify, his fury flows anew.
"You're full of anger!" he cries out, "That's all that's wrong with you!"

A top, conceited therapist sits smugly at his table
As bit by bit you try to tell what makes you feel unstable.
He does talk sense, but much success has stifled all real care,
The telephone rings constantly, he quite forgets you're there.
"Ah yes, where were we? Oh, time's up. Same time next week okay?"
"No, we've only had ten minutes and for thirty I must pay."

A well-renowned psychiatrist who's travelled far and wide,
Says wisely "Dear, you seem depressed," as, glum, you step inside.
He says no more, tells you to strip and lie upon a bed.
"What's happening, what's he up to, why do this?" flies through your head.
He soon returns and gracefully withdraws the Spring Street sheet,
Testing reflexes of knees, of arms, of shaking feet.
Not finished then, he puts his hands where you feel filled with shame.
That's bad enough, but next time too he merely does the same.

There was a really good one once; she listened, talked and cared,
And like a friend she gave support and lucid counsel shared.
A lively woman, full of courage, youngish, forty-eight?
She kept on helping people until cancer sealed her fate.

1983

THE BEGGAR

As shoppers bustled here and there,
He huddled, lonely, on the street;
A mangy dog lay by his side,
An upturned beret at his feet.
I'd seen this many times before,
So many folk whose lives were wrecked;
Their hearts and minds, their urgent need
Were blanketed by our neglect.
People hurried past this chap
As if he really wasn't there;
They didn't see the dismal coins,
His downcast look or filthy hair.
They didn't stop to ask his name
Or see if they could comfort him;
They didn't want to grasp his plight
Or why his future was so dim.
They didn't want the thought to come
That they could well be in his place,
That Lady Luck had smiled on them
But drilled despair into his face.

As for me, I felt such shame,
I put a dollar in his hand;
I could have given so much more
Or taken time to understand.
Instead I rushed to catch my bus
And wipe his memory from my head,
But late that night he haunted me
As I lay comfortably in bed.

1983

EGO

Without enough,
We skulk and stagger,
Caught in a cage of effacement.

With excess,
We strut and swagger
Trapped in a dance of dominance.

In sickness,
It strangles strength,
Eats endeavour.

In health,
It steels strength,
Loves limitlessly,
Existing incognito.

1983

CONTRAST

Not knowing need,
Food is facile.
Devoid of despair,
Hope is heartless.
Unaware, ignorant,
Understanding escapes us.
Without hell,
Heaven is unheeded.

1984

GRIEF

It can't be true although I knew
That she was going to die.
For months I have prepared myself,
Trying not to cry.

The matron has just told me
That my mother is no more.
Why is it so much worse now
Than it was the day before?

Yesterday I saw her,
She couldn't say my name;
The cancer had so eaten
And destroyed her once tall frame.

There's been so little contact
Since the time that she fell ill.
We weren't allowed to truly speak ---
"I'll get well one day, Jill."

Those endless daily visits
With the pointless conversation,
A smile upon her shrinking face
Hid inward desperation.

I would leave mechanically
My feelings tightly choked.
Folk all pretended, fearful
What a talk might have provoked.

The funeral comes, her countless friends,
Who loved her heart and soul.
I stand there blindly battling
To keep horror in control.

The next day it is over,
The crowds have disappeared.
I sit out in the sun and find
It's far worse than I'd feared.

I simply cannot comprehend
My mother is not there.
Oh God, how much I loved her
And there's no one now to care.

The future seems a futile thing
Empty beyond expression;
I feel so racked with pain and loss
Far deeper than depression.

My mother gave her heart to me,
Her I too did adore.
There's no one left who needs my love
Or loves me anymore.

The weeks pass very slowly
And I spend much time alone,
Endlessly releasing pain
That bores into my bone.

At times I feel a sense of anger,
Maybe even rage.
Why did she leave me all alone
At such a youthful age?

I look at people on the tram,
They've probably still got mothers;
They've probably got fathers too
And husbands, lovers, brothers.

I envy all the elderly ---
They'll die soon since they're old.
If only I could quell this torture,
Find someone to hold.

And so a year or more goes by,
Such loneliness and fear,
Desert, insecurity;
Where are you, mother dear?

But time will heal your wounds, they say,
And gradually you'll find
That distance ---- people, work and life
Will bring back health of mind.

And yes, it's true, things do recede,
We all must journey far,
Yet though the misery did fade
There still remains a scar.

1984

FATHER

From my earliest childhood memories on,
My father stood apart;
I loved him for his size and strength
And kindliness of heart.

Other dads seemed ordinary
Quite colourless and bland;
My father towered godlike
In my world of wonderland.

He showered me with attention,
Generosity and love,
Looking on my tiny self
Proudly from above.

At times when we went out alone
I'd shiver with delight;
He had a magic light for me,
Such power to excite.

As well he had a temper,
At times I was afraid;
His every wish, instruction
I readily obeyed.

At age fourteen I noticed
Our relationship had changed;
I questioned him, as slowly
My perceptions rearranged.

His opinions, ever rigid,
Became yet tighter, stiffer.
Confused, reluctantly I saw
Our views began to differ.

A year or two of flux flew by
And then I watched, stood still;
We realised that my temperamental
Father was now ill.

The arteries leading to his brain
Were thickening and clogged;
Without sufficient blood supply
His mind was woolly, fogged.

He grew ever more cantankerous,
Forgetful, angry, tired.
Wherever had that man gone
As a child I'd so admired?

I felt my love for him abate,
He smeared our lives with strain
As mentally he slipped away
Along a solo lane.

Unlike the love I'd used to feel.
A hatred filled my head;
And, now I'm horrified to say,
At times I wished him dead.

Too young was I to understand
His agony, alone;
And now, remorseful, I cannot
For my neglect atone.

Several years travelled,
The visitors grew fewer,
Our home became a dismal morgue
Which I could not endure.

The time arrived when Mum and I
Could cope with him no more.
With guilt we put him into care,
Our vigour to restore.

He stayed weeks there till sadly
He was placed in a closed ward,
A gruesome, ghastly place where patients
Languished lonely, bored.

The last time that I saw him
There was fear upon his face
As from his cage he crept to me ---
That look I can't erase.
And then a stroke, cremation,
So many standing by;
Yet for that man I'd fiercely loved
I couldn't even cry.

1984

HOPE

A strand
Sews human souls
Together through the centuries.
Careless of culture,
Unconscious of creed or colour,
It spurts spontaneously;
Art,
Immortal inspiration
Which guards goodness,
Wins wars
And talks of truth.

1984

SPARROW

Little bird
I love your cheek,
Your tiny form,
Your busy beak.
You hop about,
No sign of fear,
You seize a crumb,
Then disappear.
But soon you're back,
What can you find?
You hunt with joy,
You just don't mind.
You peek at me
As if to say
You'd like a treat,
Then you're away.

I watch, absorbed,
Without a word.
You fill my heart
Sweet little bird.

1984

TORCH

A teacher tells us
Where to find
Fruit.
A fight for survival
Truly
Illuminates the way
To wealth within.

1984

STATUS

Moneyed mansions
Scorn shacks.

Stuffed scholars
Ignore illiterates.

White whimps
Treat colour with contempt.

Silly sophisticates
Sneer at peasants.

Future dust
All of us.

1984

GRIT

So much abounds that chills a heart,
Aborts a faith in life,
But priceless goodness plays its part
To counter times of strife.
Bravery in horror's face
Profoundly we admire,
Images we won't erase
And memories that inspire.
Persons who deliver care
Amidst a torrid war;
Others who despite despair
Confront what lies in store.
Fearlessness in ugly places
Flares the flame of good;
Kindness in courageous faces
Links our brotherhood.

1984

CONNED

"Acquire!" we are urged,
"Consume!" the common creed
Believed by the bullied.
"No home is whole
Lacking latest luxuries.
Ride the road to riches
And reap!"

Clogged with clutter,
People pursue the promised prize;
Packed with paraphernalia,
Souls stalk serenity.

In a nameless hamlet
A host of humans huddle
Near their huts.
A fire burns,
Licking lassitude,
Binding brotherhood,
Ushering unity.

1984

BEAUTY

It often dwells
Unseen and simple,
Hiding from blind eyes:
A vivid flying scarf,
Homely cottage kitchens,
A laneway's winding charms,
Bright washing pegged out a peasant window,
A puppy at play in a public park,
Passersby graciously gathering a shopper's fruit
Strewn on the sidewalk,
The optimism in young eyes,
The wrinkled grin of an old man
Sitting in the street,
A humble dwelling where folk who love
Strive to live.

Most of all,
Kindness,
Found in the faces
Who've fought, failed, flowered
In the fray of life.

1984

GOLD

A pearl pervades,
Under-valued.
A giant gem
Building bonds,
Soothing scars,
Untrammelling tension,
Gyrating generously —
Lusty laughter.

1985

DELIGHT

Some animals engage us
With what humans hide;
Naked naturalness.

Sweetness,
Guilelessness,
Lack of pretension.

Why don't we
Who study them
Learn the core of their charm
And wear it ourselves?

1985

SOLITAIRE

No single syllable
Fosters fear, terror,
As the word
'Alone'.

Yet till we experience
Its entire embrace,
The road to what we seek
Stays barred.

1985

COMPANIONS

Deserting us only
In times of despair,
They recover
To worm their way in
And warm our weariness.
Candles of creativity,
Tendrils of hope and longing,
They flounce and flourish;
Dreams.
Fantasies
Which unleash our hearts
And flirt with us into the future.

1985

ME AND MINE

I own eleven houses,
Apartment blocks galore,
My name on countless buildings
One really can't ignore.
The sun beams on my private beach,
I stride my private links,
No limit to the wads of cash
I spend on food and drinks.
My businesses earn profits
That uphold my shiny life;
I go on lavish holidays
Joined by my busty wife.
Whatever actions I must take,
I feel no pain at all;
I've never heard the adage
That pride goes before a fall.
Other folk, they're simple pawns
For me to move about;
They've got no relevance or point
Except to give me clout.
My truck with other businessmen
I have because I must;
I've never bothered finding mates,
There's no one I can trust.
Those around me bow and scrape,
So pleased to drop my name,
Yet nothing warm connects us
And for that I feel no shame.
I'm ever earning more and more,
It's never quite enough;

My art collection needs to grow,
I want more priceless stuff.
My fingers swell around their rings,
My belly grows with wealth,
But I don't stop to worry over
Boring things like health.
And yet there is an emptiness,
Deep down a silent stress;
No cause to look more closely though,
Not something I'll address.
One day amidst much show and fuss
My glamorous life will end,
And I'll have swaggered through my days
Without a single friend.

1986

FOOLS

People can be so uncannily intelligent —
Skills, knowledge, invention, technology
Amaze in their magnitude.

And yet,
The simplest of discoveries
Continue to elude;
Feeling, without fear.
Caring, without compromise.
Living and Loving
Without Anxiety.

1986

AFTERMATH

Love
Profound, pure, total
As a well of longing,
Torn
By terrible circumstance
Into shrieking shreds.

A holocaust happened —
A heart's Hiroshima.

Now,
After the blast,
The wilderness smells sweet.
An uncharted future beckons
With unchained challenge.

Over the swollen sore of sadness
Flies freedom fearlessly,
A sense of faith.

The last barricade,
The lust for all-consuming love
Has been broken.

                                              1986

CHOICE

A fork forms.
Which way to turn?

On the left,
The simpler route
Racked with rationalisation,
We dodge through inward lies
Into doom.

On the right,
We countenance a conquest,
A tortured tunnel
Leading into light.

1986

BLANKET

This warmth
We urge through ownership,
   chase through children,
   pursue through partners.
It inhabits ourselves
Solely, softly —
Security.

1986

CHAOS

A fur-clad slender female with a tailored too-tanned face
Glides into renowned boutiques with style and polished grace.

A struggling strained young mother wearing slippers on her feet
Takes on an appalling job to help her make ends meet.

    A smug obese estate agent with huge investments, horses,
    Lounges in a bistro eating endless luscious courses.

    A bent and gnarled old fellow twists his hand into a bin,
    With half a roll or hamburger he won't be quite so thin.

A privileged young woman bears her child in 'cotton wool';
She takes it home to luxury, a costly private school.

On a street in India a baby boy is born;
The mother screams, his sisters starve, their rags are filthy, torn.

    The members of a family own several houses each,
    Priceless jewellery, shares and yachts and havens near the beach.

    Another group has scattered, the kids gone into 'care';
    There weren't sufficient funds or food or clothes for them to share.

A well-protected personage of forty-five or so
Sheds bitter tears on noticing her roses will not grow.

Far away in Lebanon reporters watch aghast;
Civilians, soldiers, children, buildings shatter from a blast.

A sweet young teacher learned and listened, loved and gave and tried;
Her virtues, gifts were boundless yet at thirty-three she died.

I know a mean old bastard who's caused torment, hunger, fear;
And do you know, that worthless coot turns ninety-two this year.

A jumbo bound for Tokyo disintegrates to ash;
A mother thanks her God because her son survived the crash.

A not-so-lucky parent gives up his God for good;
The 'sense' behind such tragedy just can't be understood.

1986

FAÇADE

How misled we are,
Wearing masks of crackless coping,
Starched smiles,
Invulnerable.

We ought to learn
That no real feeling
Flows from,
Homes to,
A human fortress.

We should see
That mutual care
Evades armour;
That only when a chink appears
Is love born.

1986

DESIRE

Yesterday I snoozed
In my drab mantle,
Impulses trimmed,
Feelings dimmed,
Dulled by normality;
Bland mind hand in hand
With daily round.

Today,
Like the roots of a wind-torn tree
Defying earth's drag,
Emotions rip their habit.

A blazing taper
Bathes awareness
In blinding light,
And newborn longing
Aches for the other.

1986

SAGE

In others' lives the signposts show
A crystal clear direction;
She should do this, he should do that —
No need for much reflection.
This couple stays together
After so much stress and strife;
That bloke abruptly goes abroad
Escaping from his life.
A young girl keeps her baby
Despite a fight to cope;
Why doesn't she let others
Give her child chance and hope?
Tormented people swallow pills
To dull their desperate pain;
If they just pulled their socks up
They'd be on their feet again!
That man who left his marriage, kids —
A heartless thing to do;
One simply could not sympathize
From any point of view.

But wait a minute, what about
The turmoil in myself?
Oh that's far worse, much harder,
I'll just put it on the shelf
Until one day I'll sit and think
And try to sort it out,
For what I'm facing's far too tough
To now be clear about.
My life lacks neat solution

Unlike lives of those I know;
They're lacking guts and insight,
I could show them where to go.

But, back to me, can I fix my
Dilemma throwing dice?
Time's passing by, I'm feeling lost,
I might just ask advice ———
No, no, my struggle's messier
Than conflicts faced by others.
It's best I wait and wisely watch
The follies of my brothers.

1986

DEATH'S DOOR (Haiku)

Tiny child so still,
Pencil wrist drip-fed softly.
Let her stay with me.

1987

ENCOUNTER

Two meet —
Rapport,
Defying reason,
Brings explosive
Intimacy.

Passion overrules inhibition;
The greatest moment pulsates —
Abandonment.

1996

WHIRLPOOL

A chance encounter
Changes all;
A past landscape
Familiar, commonplace,
Comfortable as a country field,
Transforms.

Light days of love
Soar;
Between,
Dark nights tremble.

What of tomorrow?

1996

NIRVANA

Eyes fuse,
Mouths meet,
Arms enfold,
Forms entwine.

Apart for a hundred hours,
Pent-up longing
Explodes in intimacy
No god understands.

1996

ACME

For humans,
Life reigns at random;
Triumphs and tragedies
Roll without order.
Amidst the drama
Amble common days.
And,
Now and then,
Two dance
On the roof of existence.

1996

PLUNDER

I have been pillaged.
Not long ago,
I was whole,
Intact.
Since then,
He has soaked my soul,
Drunk my desire,
Captured my consciousness.
Nothing is mine now.

1996

EDEN

Today in my garden
Bloom a million flowers;
Their vibrant colours
Flood my life.

Celebrate them
And ignore
The tall dark trees
Of tomorrow.

1996

KEEPSAKE

No matter what,
Never forget
Us.
Never let
The smoky years
Shrivel our love
To a feeble shadow.

Because
I gave you
Me;
I am ever changed.
In your distant land,
Remember always,
No matter what.

1996

THE GOVERNESS

My mum and my dad and my sister and me,
We lived in a cottage not far from the sea.
Our parents worked hard, we were often alone,
And when I say 'we' I mean just me and Joan.
We lived far away from the school and the town
So on Mondays and Fridays a teacher came down.
She came in the morning to teach Joan and me,
And if we were lucky she'd be gone before tea.
Her name was Miss Steel and it suited her well
For if we displeased her she'd stand there and yell:
"You stupid boy, Peter, you foolish girl, Joan,
Your manners are shocking, your brains are of bone."
Miss Steel was not only bad-tempered and mean,
Her face was quite truly a sight to be seen.
Her teeth were bright yellow, her nose was a hook,
The back of her head was as flat as a book
And her small piggy eyes had a hideous look.
Our dad was a fireman and often away,
He left early most mornings and stayed out all day.
Our mother made clothes she could sell in the town,
Shirts, dresses and shorts and the odd dressing gown.
If Miss Steel wasn't there Mum would call us for lunch
And give us the yummiest biscuits to munch
But on Mondays and Fridays we'd eat with Miss Steel
And watch while she gobbled her very strange meal.
She'd brought it from home in a grotty old box
Which smelt like a pile of disgusting old socks.
The food in the box was always the pits,
Raw onions and lemons and black bread in bits,
(Just watching her eat it would have us in fits.)

She piled up the onions on pieces of bread
And then like a creature who'd never been fed,
She gobbled it fast, like a pig, as I've said.
And she'd watch like a hawk as we chewed up each crust
And the skins on our fruit, oh yes they were a must.
She'd go off her head if we grumbled or fussed.
She'd scream: "You are so lucky, young Peter and Joan.
You get plenty to eat so you're not skin and bone.
If you were my children you'd learn not to moan!"
And then she'd sit down with a burp and a groan.
And now I must tell you about what she wore
On the skinniest body that I ever saw.
Her shirt had a hole and was purplish-brown,
Her skirt was so short that her undies hung down,
Her shoes were quite ancient and squeaked when she walked
And her false teeth would wiggle whenever she talked.
But the worst thing about her that I have to tell
Is that she and her clothes had this terrible smell
So that if you sat near her you wouldn't feel well.
The lessons she gave would bore us to death
As she filled up the room with her oniony breath.
She'd give us the craziest sums to work out,
They meant nothing to us, what were they about?
For example, here's one of the sums that we had.
You might not believe me because it's quite mad.
She said: "Twenty-three cats came through your front door
And seventeen stayed curled up on the floor
While three of them jumped through the window outside
And the very next morning three pussy cats died.
So how many are left? Come on, you decide!"
And so we would puzzle and think for a time
And if we were wrong, oh dear, what a crime!
Miss Steel would start snorting with anger and shout

And sometimes I feared that her teeth would fall out
As her mouth shook with rage and she'd give me a clout.
Or she'd make us read poems two hundred years old
From a dreary old book almost covered with mould
About all sorts of things we did not understand
About some crazy stuff from a far distant land,
And if we went wrong she'd say: "Put out your hand!"
I don't have to tell you what she would do then,
She'd strike with a cane, again and again
Until, ever so slowly, she'd counted to ten.

I'm sorry to say there's an end to this tale,
Not a good one, in fact it might cause you to wail.
One cold Monday morning we both lay in wait,
Our parents were gone for the day till quite late
And we'd planned for Miss Steel a most horrible fate.
I hid in the bushes behind a big tree,
A rock in my hand which I'd aim at her knee,
Then she'd crumple and fall to the ground in a heap
And I'd dig a large hole where I'd bury her, deep,
And she'd never awaken again from her sleep.
And you know it did happen; she screeched and she cried
Whilst we did all we could to make sure she had died.
That we knew what took place we completely denied
And when asked what had happened, we both outright lied.
Miss Steel simply slipped from our world and our life;
There was no one who missed her, she'd been no one's wife,
So we nurtured our secret, avoiding all strife.
The old shrew was no more in the world that we knew
(Not a kind way to bid the poor woman adieu)!

1998

MOTHERHOOD

When you were five
I used to 'pray'
That I'd survive
To see the day
That you would be
Grown up and strong,
When I could see
You sing your song;
When I could trust
That you would know
The things you must,
The way to go,
To face what comes
No matter what,
And love your chums …
They're what you've got.

You're twenty-five
Years old today;
I've watched you thrive
In your own way.
You've filled my dream
Of long ago.
My heart is full,
I love you so.

2012

LOVE

It's all we need,
A little joy,
Kind words, a hug
Our hearts to buoy.

It's all we need,
A stable link
That won't allow
Our hearts to sink.

It's all we need
If young or old;
A soul who cares,
Someone to hold.

We may be rich,
We could be poor;
What price a friend,
An open door?

And once 'undressed',
Our layers off,
There's little left
Save love, sweet love.

2013

ALL OF US

'The common man,'
'Ordinary folk,'
'The little people,'
'Man in the street.'

I've not met any
Wearing such lowly labels.
Each has his story,
A seat unlike another
In life's caravan.

2013

SONNET (To My Mother)

I lie inert amongst the grass so green
And weeping, scan the cloudless sky above,
Thou who hast my priceless treasure been,
Who poured on me an endless fount of love;
If only I could find amidst the blue
Thy face adoring, cancelling my pain,
The sweetest countenance I ever knew
Whose care so sheltered me from life's black rain.
But in my heart I know my loss won't heal
There is no balm to soothe my life bereft,
No means to fill my wish to no more feel,
Or offer meaning to my world that's left.
    If there's a God, why causeth he such woe,
    Why maketh He us mortals suffer so?

2014

HOMECOMING (Haiku)

Ears, paws, tail awhirl;
Furry welcome lights the dusk
Like no other lamp.

2014

ALPHABET POEM 1
DES(S)ERTS

A
Big
Crocodile
Decides
Eating
Fat
Greedy
Humans
Is
Just
Karma;
Likewise
Many
Naughty
Older
People
Quite
Relish
Something
Tempestuous
Unsettling
Vain
Witless
Xhibitionistic
Youthful
Zombies

2015

ALPHABET POEM 2
ANEW

A recluse
Befriended a
Companion to
Diminish his
Endless
Feeling of
Grinding
Human
Isolation.

Just Jack's
Kindness
Lulled
Miserable Mick's
Negative
Occasions
Peacefully
Quietly and
Rapidly
So
That
Unhappy
Viewpoints
Waned and
(e)Xited his (e)xistence

Yesteryear
Zonked.

2015

TECHNO FANTASY

One day, beyond my humble, blurry dreams
There may be found a tool which has the means
To note each human life each passing day
As it is lived from birth until decay.
The fun, the toil, the pain, the joy, the love,
Kaleidoscope of man, viewed from above.

No life will be ignored and each will be
Recorded in a global inventory
That paints the varied hues of all our lives
As in each time and place each person strives.
This massive lens will snap all at a glance,
Rich potpourri of human circumstance.

Meanwhile, dogs bark, the caravan moves on;
The train of life extends its marathon.
I think, I feel, I yearn, I mourn, I age,
How do I break the bars that build my cage
And find a peace that comes when I can see
Our earth in all its vast entirety?

            2014

RETAIL THERAPY

I'm strolling in a clothing store,
It gives me heaps of pleasure,
Looking at these varied garments,
Nothing made to measure.

The things I like I love to try,
My mind's allowed to wander;
Amidst the hangers, labels, racks
My worries vanish yonder.

I flit absorbed amongst the clothes
Within my shopping bubble,
Trying to avoid the urge
My credit bill to double.

But several bags are in my hand
As I depart the shop,
Till right outside a homeless man
Compels my calm to stop.

At once I feel the grip of guilt,
These goods I do not need;
Us lucky folks, we waste so much
That other mouths could feed.

I know all this, and yet I know
That I'll return one day
To give myself another treat,
My conscience locked away.

2016

WHO KNOWS

Why has the world formed thus, I ask,
And not a different way;
What's really at the root of things ---
There's no one who can say.
Why is it I'm on planet earth
And not a distant star,
Or part of Mars or Jupiter
We study from afar.
Why am I not a tiny ant
Crawling on a road,
Why not a dragonfly or horse,
An elephant or toad.
Why am I not an octopus,
A crab, a trout, a shark,
Why am I not nocturnal
Living life whilst in the dark.
I could have been a flowering plant,
A weed, a crop, a tree,
Why don't I grow amongst some rocks
Or flourish in the sea.
Why am I not a piece of wood,
A table leg, a chair,
What fun to be a crimson kite
Free-flying in the air,
Or maybe just a puff of wind,
A foaming ocean wave,
A gleaming ray of sunlight
Or a stone on someone's grave.

How is it I'm a human
And a she and not a he;
How is it I'm the way I am,
Why is it that I'm me?

2016

REGRET

The day was calm and light
But my heart felt dark and tight;
I knew that I must travel to the lake.
It was years since I had been,
So very long since I'd been keen
The journey to that haunted place to make.

I thought about the past,
That day which shadows cast,
That moment that resulted from a whim;
We'd pinched a neighbour's car
And dreamed of driving far
Till Dave announced a stop so we could swim.

The lake was shining blue,
A big oak beside it grew
And plucky Dave climbed out along a bough.
I begged him to take care
But he took it as a dare
and shouted out: "Just watch! I'm diving now."

In a trice the world turned leaden,
I felt all my being deaden
For already I had grasped this story's end.
That exultant, youthful leap
Into waters five feet deep
Had fixed a dreadful fate for my best friend.

There's not much more to say
About the horror of that day,

But Dave and I, we never spoke again.
He left us all behind,
His passing scarred my mind
And condemned me to a manhood full of pain.

So today I would return
To that sad lagoon to learn
If I could ease my guilt and find some peace.
It was time for me to face
The gnawing darkness of that place,
Though the missing of my mate would never cease.

2016

THE LAST EVENING

We sit alone. He's very still.
No threats. No sound at all.
A stranger, quieter evening
I simply can't recall.

My anxious thoughts are thumping,
I fear they can be heard;
What if he gleans my project
As we sit without a word?

What if he draws awareness
From the terror deep in me?
What if he's figured out
That in the morning I will flee?

He's sitting fiddling with his phone
While I pretend to read;
If he could read my restless mind
All would be lost indeed.

At morning light he'll leave for work
And I will rush away.
Our past has mutilated me,
I simply cannot stay.

I've packed a few essentials,
Got a ticket well concealed;
I've been so patient, careful,
So my plan won't be revealed.

For once he isn't drinking,
I'm scared that he might know;
What if he's working out a way
To thwart my plan to go?

At last he coughs and leaves the room,
He makes his way to bed.
If I don't escape tomorrow
Then I know I'll soon be dead.

2016

BROKEN

A host of human creatures,
Each alone;
Needing to connect yet
On their own.

To this vast house of respite
Doctors came,
Medicating patients
Without name.

Activities were programmed,
Mealtimes shared,
But what most wanted was that
Someone cared.

The doors revolved as inmates
Came and went,
The E.C.T. machine did
Not relent.

A grey, grim girl stayed silent,
Fingers stained;
Just cigarettes her lover-----
Nothing gained.

Another lay in bed, she
Never rose;
The endless round of drugs
Entrenched her woes.

Beyond this place were lives of
Greater luck,
Where life's wild whims brought love
And dreams, unstuck.

But here, folk floundered, faded,
Wept inside;
Their link to life, their hopes
Had all but died.

So many human creatures
On their own;
Each heart born full of life-----
Where had it gone?

2016

TIME OUT

Enfolding night
Immense and deep;
If fate is kind,
A troubled mind
Is soothed by sleep
In soft oblivion.

Till shards of light
And stirring sound
Rip rest apart,
Tear dormant heart;
Old torment found
As day dawns.

2016

WASTE LAND

Here, silent people sleep.
They cannot speak their truth
Or hear the words
We should have spoken.
They cannot feel the love
We could have shown.
Their wealth, rotting,
Feeds the weeds swarming
Without respect,
Wantonly across their wisdom.
Such waste of vivid lives
Oft too soon severed,
Sloughed from the stream.

Our tears cannot tempt them
To help us heal,
Or ease our emptiness.
We are strangers now,
Evermore unknown to them
In their oblivion.

2016

EXIT

I'm really not afraid of death,
Not death itself that is;
What scares me is what goes before ...
That puts me in a tizz.
Let me avoid a high care home
Where I'm no longer me,
Where 'nurses' without training
Do not see my misery.
They won't know how to treat my pain,
Or calm my life, bereft;
They simply won't have time or care
To soothe what days are left.
And what if it went on for years,
That thought fills me with dread,
The image of me lying, helpless,
Stuck each day in bed.
And if some people visited
To show their love and care,
They'd not know my reality,
My horror or despair.
The manager would reassure,
Their ears with comfort fill.
"Don't worry. All is well," she'd say.
"We take good care of Jill."

I will not let another soul
Tell me when I can die.
Ideas, faiths of other folk
Won't me my choice deny.
Nor will I hand them all my cash
To fund that living death.
No, I will die with dignity
In charge till my last breath.

2016

www.ingramcontent.com/pod-product-compliance
Lightning Source LLC
Chambersburg PA
CBHW071026080526
44587CB00015B/2520